My
FAVORITE
PRAYERS

STORMIE
OMARTIAN

HARVEST HOUSE PUBLISHERS
EUGENE, OREGON

MY FAVORITE PRAYERS
Copyright © 2015 by Stormie Omartian
Published by Harvest House Publishers
Eugene, Oregon 97402
www.harvesthousepublishers.com

ISBN 978-0-7369-6343-5 (pbk.)
ISBN 978-0-7369-6344-2 (eBook)

ontents

Lord, Shine Your Light on Every Step I Take
5–20

Lord, Help Me Love My Husband by Praying for Him
21–36

Lord, I Lift Up My Life to You
37–50

Lord, Teach Me to Be Mighty in Prayer
51–66

Lord, I Want to Be a Great Parent
67–82

Lord, Show Me How to Pray for My Grown-Up Kids
83–98

Lord, Thank You for the Presence of
Your Spirit in My Life
99–114

Lord, I Want to Reflect Your Heart
115–130

Lord, Help Me Love You and Others
in a Way That Pleases You
131–144

Introduction

❧❦❧

I have often been asked what my favorite prayers are of all those in my books. So I have collected the ones that have been most important to me personally, as well as prayers others said meant the most to them.

I pray they will bless *you* as well.

Stormie Omartian

Lord,
Shine Your Light on
Every Step I Take

(Prayers from *Just Enough Light
for the Step I'm On*)

Learning to Walk

Lord, I don't want to take one step without You. I reach up for Your hand and ask that You lead me in Your way. Thank You that no matter where I am right now, even if I have gotten way off course, in this moment as I put my hand in Yours, You will make a path from where I am to where I need to be. And You will lead me on it. I love that Your grace abounds to me in that way. Keep me on the path You have for me and take me where You want me to go. I commit this day to walking with You. Thank You, Lord, that You are teaching me how to walk in total dependence upon You, for I know therein lies my greatest blessing.

In Jesus' name I pray.

Beginning to See the Light

~∿~

Lord, You are the light of my life. You illuminate my path, and I will follow wherever You lead. Protect me from being blinded by the light that confuses. Help me to always identify the counterfeit. I depend on You to lift up the light of Your countenance upon me (Psalm 4:6). Thank You, Lord, that because You never change, Your light is constant in my life no matter what is going on around me. Shine Your light through me as I walk with my hand in Yours. I give this day to You and trust that the light You give me is just the amount I need for the step I'm on. I acknowledge that You are the true Light who gives light to the world (John 1:9). Thank You that Your light will never be put out, and I can never really be in darkness when I look to You.

In Jesus' name I pray.

Refusing to Be Afraid of the Dark

❧

Lord, thank You that because I walk with You I don't have to fear the dark. Even in the blackest night, You are there. In the darkest times, You have treasures for me. No matter what I am going through, Your presence and grace are my comfort and my light. Your Word says, "If one walks in the night, he stumbles, because the light is not in him" (John 11:9,10). But I know Your light *is* in me. Jesus, You have come as a light into the world so that whoever believes in You should not abide in darkness (John 12:46). Thank You that as I take each step, the light You give me will be all I need.

In Jesus' name I pray.

Embracing the Moment

*L*ord, help me to embrace the moments of my life that are hard to get my arms around. Enable my eyes to see You in them. Help me to always acknowledge the abundance of Your goodness to me. I lift to You the deepest struggles in my life. I trust You to open my eyes to see all You have for me in them. Reveal to me the fullness of it all. Thank You that I can be filled with the joy of Your presence in every step I take because You have given me the light I need for whatever step I am on. Help me to have a greater sense of Your presence every day.

In Jesus' name I pray.

Dancing in the Footlights

*L*ord, shine the light of Your Word on the path of my life today. Make it a lamp for my feet so that I do not stumble. Bring it alive in my spirit so that it illuminates my mind and soul. Let it be a guide for every decision I make, every step I take. Keep me from turning to the right or the left so that I will stay on the narrow path that leads to life. Help me daily to carve out time to be alone with You and to feed on Your truth. Align my heart with Yours and give me revelation and guidance so that I can know Your will for my life. Shine the lamp of truth where I am right now and show me the next step to take.

In Jesus' name I pray.

See What's Right with This Picture

~~~

Lord, I lay my worries before You and ask for Your mighty intervention to show me what's right when I can only see what's wrong. I am determined to see the good, so help me not to be blinded by my own fears, doubts, wants, and preconceived ideas. I ask You to reveal to me Your truth in every situation. Bless me with the ability to understand the bigger picture and to distinguish the valuable from the unimportant. When something seems to go wrong, help me not to jump to negative conclusions. Enable me to recognize the answers to my own prayers. I trust You to help me see the light in every situation. I rejoice this day and every day because You are in charge of them all.

In Jesus' name I pray.

Believing It's Not Over Till It's Over

Lord, my times are in Your hands. Thank You that my life is never over here on this earth until You say it is. And when that time comes, I will see You face-to-face and dwell in Your presence. Thank You that You never give up on me, even when I have given up on myself. I am so happy that no matter what age I am, I will always have purpose because You have great things for me to do. I pray that You would give me an ever-renewing sense of Your purpose for my life. Use me for Your glory as long as I am on this earth. Help me to never be resistant to change, but instead to always be open to new things You want to do.

In Jesus' name I pray.

Surviving Disappointment

~~~~~~~

*L*ord, in times of great disappointment I will cling to You. As I walk through those times, teach me what You want me to learn. Reveal Your truth to me in every situation. Help me to see it clearly for what it really is. Keep me from fretting over my circumstances or living in unforgiveness regarding them. I want to, instead, wait in Your presence for You to reveal Your goodness to me in the situation. I want to always rest in You, knowing my life is in Your hands. I put You in charge of every detail of my life, even the pain I feel in my heart. Use it to perfect me and bring glory to You. Thank You for Your endless goodness toward me.

In Jesus' name I pray.

Traveling Through the Dark Moments of Relationships

~∞~

Lord, shine Your light of revelation into every relationship I have and show me Your truth. Illuminate any darkness of unforgiveness in me, and I will confess it to You as sin. Bring reconciliation and clarity in place of misunderstanding. Where I need to humbly extend myself, enable me to make any necessary sacrifice and not cater to the cries of my flesh. Help me to lay down my life in prayer for my family, friends, and others You have put in my life. Teach me how to love the way that You do. I join my hand in Yours as I travel the path of relationships with Your unconditional love as my guiding light. Help me to be unselfish as I look out for the interests of others.

In Jesus' name I pray.

Walking in the Midst of the Overwhelming

～⁓ⁿ◈ⁿ⁓～

*L*ord, I can only make it through this time if I walk closely with You. While there are many things that can happen in life that are frightening or overwhelming, I know that Your power is greater than all of them. Even when what I experience is too much for me, it is never too much for You. Anything I face is nothing alongside Your ability to redeem it. Lord, I lift to You the things that frighten me most and ask that You would protect me and the people I love from them. Specifically, I bring before You (name of overwhelming situation) and ask that You would work Your redemption in it. Give me a deeper sense of Your presence, for I know that Your presence is far greater than anything I might fear.

In Jesus' name I pray.

Reaching for God's Hand in Times of Loss

~~~

Lord, enable me to get beyond any sorrow or grief I feel in my life. I realize life must go on, and I ask You to help me take the next step I need to take today. Even though it may be hard to imagine life without the pain I feel, with You all things are possible. Your healing power can restore anything—even a broken heart. Help me to cast my whole burden of grief on You and let You carry it. Even though there are times when it feels like I can't live through the pain, I know You will sustain me. Walk with me, Lord. I trust You to take my hand and lead me until I can feel Your light on my face and joy in my heart once again.

In Jesus' name I pray.

Stepping Out of the Past

〜✦〜

*L*ord, help me to be renewed in the spirit of my mind. Where I have made wrong choices in the past, I pray that You would forgive me and redeem those mistakes. Help me to forgive myself so that I don't keep replaying them in my thoughts. Take all of my past failures and use them for good today. I know that because I have put You in charge of my future, I don't have to fear that the events of my past will keep me from moving into all You have for me. Give me Your revelation and show me all I need to see in order to walk out of the shadow of my past and into the light You have for me.

In Jesus' name I pray.

Maintaining a Passion for the Present

Lord, I realize there is no better time than the present to be Your light extended to those around me. Help me to get beyond myself and become an open vessel through which Your light can shine. Give me Your wisdom and revelation, and show me all I need to see to keep me on the road You have for me. Enable me to step out of my past and keep an eye on the future by following Your light on my path today. If You're not moving me, I'm staying here until I have a leading from You. I know I can only get to the future You have for me by walking one step at a time in Your will today.

In Jesus' name I pray.

Moving into Your Future

Lord, I ask You to be in charge of my future. I don't want to dream dreams if You are not in them. I don't want to make plans that You will not bless. I don't want to work hard trying to harvest something that will never bear fruit because I did not receive the seed from You. Help me not to waste valuable time getting off the path and having to come back to the same place again. I don't want to get to the end of my life and regret the time I spent not living for You. I want it said that Your glory was seen in my life. I trust my future to You, knowing You have it safely in Your hands.

In Jesus' name I pray.

Lord,
Help Me Love My Husband by Praying for Him

(Prayers from *The Power of
a Praying* ® *Wife*)

His Wife

*L*ord, help me to be a good wife. I realize I don't have what it takes to be one without Your help. Take my selfishness, impatience, and irritability and turn them into kindness, long-suffering, and the willingness to bear all things. Take my old emotional habits, mind-sets, automatic reactions, rude assumptions, and self-protectiveness, and make me patient, kind, good, faithful, gentle, and self-controlled. Take the hardness of my heart and break down the walls with Your battering ram of revelation. Give me a new heart and work in me Your love, peace, and joy (Galatians 5:22-23). I am not able to rise above who I am at this moment. Only You can transform me.

In Jesus' name I pray.

His Work

Lord, I pray You would bless the work of my husband's hands. May his labor bring not only favor, success, and prosperity, but great fulfillment as well. If the work he is doing is not in line with Your perfect will for his life, reveal it to him. Show him what he should do differently and guide him down the right path. Give him strength, faith, and a vision for the future so he can rise above any propensity for laziness. May he never run from work out of fear, selfishness, or a desire to avoid responsibility. On the other hand, help him to see that he doesn't have to work himself to death for man's approval. Give him the ability to enjoy his success without striving for more. Help him to excel, but free him from the pressure to do so.

In Jesus' name I pray.

His Finances

Lord, I pray my husband will have wisdom to handle money wisely. Help him make good decisions as to how he spends. Show him how to plan for the future. Teach him to give as You have instructed in Your Word. I pray he will find the perfect balance between spending needlessly and being miserly. May he always be paid well for the work he does, and may his money not be stolen, lost, devoured, destroyed, or wasted. Multiply it so that what he makes will go a long way. I pray he will not be anxious about finances, but will seek Your kingdom first, knowing that as he does, we will have all we need (Luke 12:31).

In Jesus' name I pray.

His Mind

Lord, I pray my husband will not entertain confusion in his mind, but will live in clarity. Keep him from being tormented with impure, evil, negative, or sinful thoughts. Enable him to be transformed by the renewing of his mind (Romans 12:2). Help him to be anxious for nothing, but in everything by prayer and supplication, with thanksgiving, let his requests be made known to You; and may Your peace, which surpasses all understanding, guard his heart and mind through Christ Jesus (Philippians 4:6-7). And, finally, whatever things are true, noble, just, pure, lovely, of good report, having virtue, or anything praiseworthy, let him think on these things (Philippians 4:8).

In Jesus' name I pray.

His Fears

Lord, I pray that my husband will acknowledge You as a Father whose love is unfailing, whose strength is without equal, and in whose presence there is nothing to fear. Deliver him this day from fear that destroys and replace it with godly fear (Jeremiah 32:40). Teach him Your way, O Lord. Help him to walk in Your truth. Unite his heart to fear Your name (Psalm 86:11). May he have no fear of men, but rise up and boldly say, "The Lord is my helper; I will not fear. What can man do to me?" (Hebrews 13:6). "How great is Your goodness, which You have laid up for those who fear You" (Psalm 31:19).

In Jesus' name I pray.

His Purpose

Lord, I pray my husband will clearly hear the call You have on his life. Help him to realize who he is in Christ and give him certainty he was created for a high purpose. Enable him to walk worthy of his calling and remind him of what You've called him to be. Don't let him get sidetracked with things that are unessential to Your purpose. Strike down discouragement so it will not defeat him. Lift his eyes above the circumstances of the moment so he can see the purpose for which You created him. Give him patience to wait for Your perfect timing. I pray that the desires of his heart will not be in conflict with the desires of Yours. May he seek You for direction and hear when You speak to his soul.

In Jesus' name I pray.

His Choices

Lord, fill my husband with the fear of the Lord and give him wisdom for every decision he makes. May he reverence You and Your ways and seek to know Your truth. Give him discernment to make decisions based on Your revelation. Help him to make godly choices and keep him from doing anything foolish. I pray that he will listen to godly counselors and not be a man who is unteachable. Instruct him even as he is sleeping (Psalm 16:7), and in the morning I pray he will do what's right rather than follow the leading of his own flesh. May he not buy into the foolishness of this world, but keep his eyes on You and have ears to hear Your voice.

In Jesus' name I pray.

His Reputation

Lord, I pray my husband will have a reputation that is untarnished. I know a man is often valued "by what others say of him" (Proverbs 27:21), so I pray he will be respected in our town and people will speak highly of him. You've said in Your Word that "a curse without cause shall not alight" (Proverbs 26:2). I pray there would never be any reason for bad things to be said of him. Keep him out of legal entanglements. Protect us from lawsuits and criminal proceedings. Deliver him from his enemies, O God. Defend him from those who rise up to do him harm (Psalm 59:1). In You, O Lord, we put our trust. Let us never be put to shame (Psalm 71:1).

In Jesus' name I pray.

His Past

∼◦⟡◦∽

Lord, I pray You would enable my husband
to let go of his past completely. Deliver him
from any hold it has on him. Help him to put off his
former conduct and habitual ways of thinking about
it and be renewed in his mind (Ephesians 4:22-23).
Enlarge his understanding to know that You make all
things new (Revelation 21:5). Show him a fresh, Holy
Spirit-inspired way of relating to negative things that
have happened. Give him the mind of Christ so that
he can clearly discern Your voice from the voices of
the past. When he hears those old voices, enable him
to rise up and shut them down with the truth of Your
Word.

In Jesus' name I pray.

His Attitude

~~~~~~

*L*ord, fill my husband with Your love and peace today. May there be a calmness, serenity, and sense of well-being established in him because his life is God-controlled rather than flesh-controlled. Help him to be anxious for nothing, but give thanks in all things so he can know the peace that passes all understanding. Enable him to walk in his house with a clean and perfect heart before You (Psalm 101:2). Shine the light of Your Spirit upon him and fill him with Your love. I pray he will be kind and patient, not selfish or easily provoked. Release him from anger, unrest, anxiety, concerns, inner turmoil, strife, and pressure. Enable him to bear all things, believe all things, hope all things, and endure all things (1 Corinthians 13:7).

In Jesus' name I pray.

His Self-Image

~∽∽∽~

*L*ord, I pray my husband will find his identity in You. Help him to understand his worth through Your eyes and by Your standards. May he recognize the unique qualities You've placed in him and be able to appreciate them. Enable him to see himself the way You see him, understanding that "You have made him a little lower than the angels, and You have crowned him with glory and honor. You have made him to have dominion over the works of Your hands; You have put all things under his feet" (Psalm 8:4-6). Quiet the voices that tell him otherwise and give him ears to hear Your voice telling him that it will not be his perfection that gets him through life successfully—it will be Yours.

In Jesus' name I pray.

His Faith

Lord, I pray You will give my husband an added measure of faith today. Enlarge his ability to believe in You, Your Word, Your promises, Your ways, and Your power. Put a longing in his heart to talk with You and hear Your voice. Give him an understanding of what it means to bask in Your presence and not just ask for things. May he seek You, rely totally upon You, be led by You, put You first, and acknowledge You in everything he does. Lord, You have said in Your Word that "whatever is not from faith is sin" (Romans 14:23). May my husband be free from the sin of doubt in his life.

In Jesus' name I pray.

His Hearing

ord, Your Word says that "he who has ears to hear, let him hear!" (Matthew 11:15). I pray You would give my husband ears to hear You speaking to his heart. Help him to "incline" his ears toward You at all times (Proverbs 22:17). Enable him to listen as You speak to him through Your Word and through Your Holy Spirit impressing his heart and mind. Open his ears to not only hear You but to hear me as well. Enable me to hear from You at all times and continually grow in wisdom and discernment. When I need to say something important to him, prepare his heart to receive it without pride, rejection, or disregard for the fact that You have made us to be one.

In Jesus' name I pray.

His Future

Lord, I pray You would give my husband a vision for his future. Help him to understand that Your plans for him are good and not evil—to give him a future and a hope (Jeremiah 29:11). Fill him with the knowledge of Your will in all wisdom and spiritual understanding so that he may have a walk worthy of You, fully pleasing You, being fruitful in every good work and increasing in the knowledge of You (Colossians 1:9-10). May he live by the leading of the Holy Spirit and not walk in doubt and fear of what may happen. Help him to mature and grow in You daily, submitting to You all his dreams and desires, knowing that "the things which are impossible with men are possible with God" (Luke 18:27).

In Jesus' name I pray.

Lord,
I Lift Up My Life
to You

(Prayers from *30 Days to Becoming a Woman of Prayer*)

Know Who
Your Father Is

❧

Heavenly Father, I thank You that You have given me the right to become Your child (John 1:12). Help me to live in Your love and comprehend the depth of Your care and concern for me. Take away any barrier that keeps me from fully understanding what it means to trust You as my heavenly Father. Help me to take on a family resemblance so that I have Your eyes, Your heart, and Your mind. Lord, show me any way in which I need to forgive my earthly father. Heal anything in my heart that has caused me to see You through his failings. Forgive me if I have judged Your perfection by his imperfections. Show me what I need to see, and help me to completely forgive.

In Jesus' name I pray.

Receive All Jesus Died
for You to Have

❧

 ord Jesus, I know You came "to seek and
   to save that which was lost" (Luke 19:10).
Thank You that You saw my lost condition and have
saved me for Yourself and Your purposes. Thank You
that because You died for me, I have eternal life and
your blood cleanses me from all sin (1 John 1:7). Now
I can live free of guilt and condemnation. I believe
"there is no other name under heaven" by which I
could ever be saved (Acts 4:12). Enable me to live
like the new creation You have made me to be. Thank
You, Jesus, that I am a joint heir with You of all our
Father God's blessings. Thank You for reconciling me
to Yourself (2 Corinthians 5:18).

In Jesus' name I pray.

Welcome the Holy Spirit's Presence

❧

*L*ord, teach me everything I need to know about You. Enable me to exhibit faithfulness, gentleness, and self-control (Galatians 5:22-23). You are the Spirit of wisdom, grace, holiness, and life. You are the Spirit of counsel, might, and knowledge (Isaiah 11:2). Spirit of truth, help me to know the truth in all things. Thank You for leading and guiding me. Thank You for being my Helper and Comforter. Thank You that Your Spirit within me enables me to walk in Your ways and do Your commands (Ezekiel 36:27). Help me to pray powerfully and worship You in a way that is pleasing to You. Thank You that You will raise me up to be with You when my life on earth has ended. Until then, lead me ever closer to You.

In Jesus' name I pray.

Take God at His Word

Lord, I am grateful for Your Word. It shows me how to live, and I realize my life only works if I'm living Your way. Meet me there in the pages and teach me what I need to know. "Open my eyes, that I may see wondrous things from Your law" (Psalm 119:18). Thank You for the comfort, healing, deliverance, and peace Your Word brings me. It is food for my starving soul. Help me to read it every day so that I have a solid understanding of who You are, who You made me to be, and how I am to live. May Your words live in me so that when I pray, I will see answers to my prayers (John 15:7).

In Jesus' name I pray.

Make Worship a Habit

❧

Lord, I enter Your gates with thanksgiving, and Your courts with praise (Psalm 100:4). I worship You as the almighty, all-powerful God of heaven and earth, and the Creator of all things. No one is greater than You. I praise You as my heavenly Father, who is with me every day to guide and protect me. Thank You for all You have given me and all You will provide for me in the future. "You guard all that is mine. The land You have given me is a pleasant land" (Psalm 16:5-6 NLT). I praise You for Your love that liberates me and makes me whole. Pour Your love into me so that it overflows to others and glorifies You in the process.

In Jesus' name I pray.

Live in the Freedom God Has for You

Lord, I thank You that You are "my fortress, my high tower and my deliverer, my shield and the One in whom I take refuge" (Psalm 144:2). Thank You that "You have delivered my soul from death" and have "kept my feet from falling," so that I may walk before You (Psalm 56:13). Show me anything I need to be set free from. I don't want to be living with something from which You already paid the price for me to be liberated. I pray You "will deliver me from every evil work and preserve me" for Your kingdom (2 Timothy 4:18). "O God, do not be far from me; O my God, make haste to help me!" (Psalm 71:12).

In Jesus' name I pray.

Recognize Your Purpose and Work to Fulfill It

⚬⟋⟍⚬

*L*ord, I commit my work to You. I pray I will always be in Your will in whatever I do, and that I will do it well. I pray that all I do is pleasing to You and to those for whom and with whom I am working. Establish the work of my hands for Your pleasure and Your glory (Psalm 90:17). Help me to understand what is the hope of my calling (Ephesians 1:17-18). Enable me to "be steadfast, immovable, always abounding in the work of the Lord" that You have given me to do, knowing that my "labor is not in vain in the Lord"—as long as it is from You and for You (1 Corinthians 15:58).

In Jesus' name I pray.

Bask in God's Love

*L*ord, fill my heart with Your love in greater measure so I can be the whole person You created me to be. Give me Your heart of love for others. I pray I will be so filled with Your love that it overflows to other people in a way they can perceive it. Show me the loving thing to do in every situation. How grateful I am that nothing can separate me from Your love, no matter where I go or what I do—not even my own failings (Romans 8:35-39). Thank You that because of Your love for me, I am more than a conqueror (Romans 8:37). Thank You, Lord, that Your unfailing love and mercy surround me because I trust in You (Psalm 32:10).

In Jesus' name I pray.

Put Your Hope in the Lord

Lord, in You I put all my hope and expectations. "I will hope continually, and will praise You yet more and more" (Psalm 71:14). I know I have no hope without You (Ephesians 2:12), so my hope is entirely in You (Psalm 39:7). "For You are my hope, O Lord God; You are my trust from my youth" (Psalm 71:5). In the times I am tempted to feel hopeless—especially when I don't see answers to my prayers for a long time and I become discouraged—help me to put my eyes back on You. Enable me to end all feelings of hopelessness in my life. Help me to see they are not true and that only Your Word is true.

In Jesus' name I pray.

Give God's Way—to Him and to Others

Lord, I don't want to stop up the flow of Your blessings in my life by not giving when and where I should. I am grateful for all You have given me, but I pray I will not merely give to get, but give only to please You. Help me to understand the release that happens in my life when I give, so that I can let go of things. Help me to "not forget to do good and to share," for I know that with such sacrifices, You are "well pleased" (Hebrews 13:16). Help me to give and thereby store up treasures in heaven that do not fail, for I know that where my treasure is, my heart will be there also (Luke 12:33-34).

In Jesus' name I pray.

Stand Strong in Tough Times

━━━❦━━━

ord, thank You for helping me stand strong. You have armed me with strength for the battle (Psalm 18:39). So many times "I would have lost heart, unless I had believed that I would see the goodness of the LORD in the land of the living" (Psalm 27:13). Help me to become so strong in You that I can stand without wavering, no matter what happens. Teach me to rest in You, knowing You will give me what I need for the moment I am in. I am determined to "count it all joy" when I go through trials, because of the perfecting work You will do for me (James 1:2-4). "Though I walk in the midst of trouble, You will revive me" (Psalm 138:7).

In Jesus' name I pray.

Refuse to Give Up

Lord, my hope is in You, and I know You will never fail me. Thank You that Your restoration is ongoing in my life. I am grateful that I am Your child and You have given me purpose. Thank You for the great future You have for me because You love me (1 Corinthians 2:9). Thank You that I am complete in You (Colossians 2:10). Thank You that I am never alone (Matthew 28:20). Help me to not think of giving up when things become difficult. Help me to remember that even in hard times You will help me persevere. Keep me from becoming discouraged in times of waiting. I know Your timing is perfect and the way You do things is right.

In Jesus' name I pray.

Lord,
Teach Me to Be Mighty in Prayer

(Prayers from *Prayer Warrior*)

Understand There Is a War and You Are in It

～◦⊱⊰◦～

Lord, I pray You will help me build my life on a solid foundation. I know there is no more solid foundation than that which is built on the Rock—which is You, Jesus, and Your Word (1 Corinthians 3:11). No matter what is shaking around me, You give me a foundation that can never be shaken or destroyed. Help me to always keep in mind that I am instrumental in the war between You and Your enemy, and victory in my life depends on my willingness to hear Your call to pray. I know this is spiritual warfare You want me to engage in, and prayer *is* the battle. Teach me, Lord, to hear Your call and to pray in power the way You want me to.

In Jesus' name I pray.

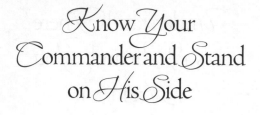

Know Your Commander and Stand on His Side

*L*ord, teach me how to be the powerful prayer warrior You have called me to be. Show me how I should pray. Enable me to take dominion over the works of darkness and take back territory the enemy has stolen from me and the rest of Your people. Help me to stand strong in prayer against the encroachment of the enemy into my life, as well as the lives of others. Enable me to serve You, being led by Your Holy Spirit in prayer. Thank You, Lord, that You will protect me and those for whom I pray. Thank You for sharing Your power with me so that I can win each battle and defeat the enemy.

In Jesus' name I pray.

Recognize Who Your True Enemy Is

⁕

*L*ord, I thank You that You have given us everything we need to stand strong against the enemy of our soul. It is You "who gives us the victory through our Lord Jesus Christ" (1 Corinthians 15:57). I acknowledge You as my Commander, and I submit myself to You as Your servant. Help me to serve You in prayer as You have asked me to do. Enable me to oppose the plans of the enemy in prayer. Whenever he tries to cause confusion in my life, I pray You will cause confusion in *his* camp when I pray. I know the enemy is no match for You, and the only way he gains power is by deceiving people into believing his lies. Keep me from all deception.

In Jesus' name I pray.

Be Certain of Your Authority in Prayer

*ord, help me to be the most effective prayer warrior possible. Teach me to understand the authority You have given me in prayer. Enable me to use that authority to break down strongholds the enemy would attempt to erect in my life and in the lives of others whom You put on my heart. Keep me from doubt that I am qualified to do this because only *You* supply me with everything I need in order to pray in power. I take my orders from You and no other. I have authority because I have You. Enable me, Holy Spirit, to always hear Your call to pray. Teach me to rest fully on the authority You have given me as Your prayer warrior.

In Jesus' name I pray.

Put On
Your Protective Armor
Each Morning

*L*ord, help me to put on the full spiritual armor You have provided for me so that I can "stand against the wiles of the devil" every day (Ephesians 6:11). Help me to put on the breastplate of righteousness that protects me from the enemy's attacks. I know it is Your righteousness *in* me that protects me, but I also know I must not neglect to put on Your righteousness like a bulletproof vest by doing what is right in Your eyes. Show me what I have done, or am *about* to do, that does not glorify You. I want to see anything in me that violates Your high standards for my life so I can confess it, turn away from it, and be cleansed from all unrighteousness.

In Jesus' name I pray.

Become Skilled with Your Spiritual Weapons

*L*ord, help me to understand what my spiritual weapons are and to become proficient in the use of them. Teach me so I don't forget for even a moment how powerful they are. Grow my faith to believe You and Your Word without doubt. I know that as the heavens are higher than the earth, so are Your ways higher than my ways, and Your thoughts higher than my thoughts (Isaiah 55:9). Help me to think and act more like You every time I read Your Word and spend time in Your presence. Enable me to know Your Word so well that I have Scriptures in my mind and heart that become automatic weapons against the enemy of my soul.

In Jesus' name I pray.

See What's Happening from God's Perspective

Lord, just as You endured the cross and the suffering that went with it because You saw the glory and joy set before You at the right hand of Your Father God, help me to endure what I must for the joy set before me of knowing You have defeated the enemy and I will spend eternity with You. Thank You for the joy of knowing we win because You have conquered death and defeated hell. I thank You that You have given me a second chance to do something great for You. No matter what I have done or what has happened in my past, You will still use me for Your purposes because I have committed my life to You in every way.

In Jesus' name I pray.

Prayer for a Covering of Protection

—◦⟡◦—

Lord, I ask You to cover me and my family with Your protection. Surround us with Your angels to keep us from danger, accidents, disease, or any plans of the enemy to harm us. You are my strength and my shield and I trust in You (Psalm 28:7). Thank You that You keep me from harm and will watch over my coming and going both now and in eternity (Psalm 121:8). "You are my hiding place and my shield; I hope in Your word" (Psalm 119:114). Thank You, Lord, that You "will bless the righteous; with favor You will surround him as with a shield" (Psalm 5:12). Thank You that in the time of trouble You will hide me from the enemy in a secret place.

In Jesus' name I pray.

Prayer for Healing

❦

*L*ord, I thank You that You are the God who heals. Thank You, Jesus, that You have "borne our griefs and carried our sorrows" and You were "wounded for our transgressions" and "bruised for our iniquities" and by Your "stripes we are healed" (Isaiah 53:4-5). Thank You that You "took our infirmities and bore our sicknesses" (Matthew 8:17). By the authority given me in the name of Jesus, I pray for healing for (<u>name of person who needs healing</u>). I pray that no plans of the enemy for this person's destruction will succeed. Bring healing to every part of her (his, my) body. Whether this infirmity is healed instantly or requires a convalescent period, I give You the glory as our Creator and Healer.

In Jesus' name I pray.

Prayer for Provision

⁓ ❧ ⁓

Lord, I know the enemy can use our finances as a point of attack, so I want to cover them in prayer. I submit myself and my finances and all I have to You. Thank You for the many blessings You have given me. Help me to glorify You in all I do with everything I have. I know all good things come from You. Help me to please You in my paying, giving, buying, and spending. Your Word says that "the blessing of the LORD makes one rich, and He adds no sorrow with it" (Proverbs 10:22). I pray that the enemy cannot rob and steal from me or my family. Help us to be good stewards of all You have given us.

In Jesus' name I pray.

Prayer for Others to Be Saved

❦

Lord, You have said, "I am the door. If anyone enters by Me, he will be saved, and will go in and out and find pasture" (John 10:9). "I give them eternal life, and they shall never perish; neither shall anyone snatch them out of My hand" (John 10:28). I pray that the people I lift up before You will walk through that door into eternal life and will not be snatched out of Your hand. Help them to hear Your Word and believe it. I pray that even now they cannot be blinded and taken from You by the enemy. I claim them for Your kingdom. Help them to know Your greatest gift to us, which is eternal life with You.

In Jesus' name I pray.

Prayer for Strength in the Battle

⁓◦∽∾◦⁓

*L*ord, I thank You that "You have armed me with strength for the battle; You have subdued under me those who rose against me" (2 Samuel 22:40). Lord, may Your strength be made perfect in my weakness (2 Corinthians 12:9). I pray that Your power will rest on me, for You are my strength. You are the "strength of my life; of whom shall I be afraid?" (Psalm 27:1). I pray You will pull me out of any net the enemy has laid for me because I rely on Your strength (Psalm 31:4). The specific battle I am facing now is (name the battle you are facing). Help me to stand strong with Your armor on and the weapons You have given me ready to be used.

In Jesus' name I pray.

Prayer for Deliverance and Freedom

~~~

*L*ord, I know the enemy wants us all to live in condemnation, but You set us free from our sins and the consequences of them if we confess them before You. Thank You that if I confess my sins, You are faithful and just to forgive my sin and to cleanse me from all unrighteousness (1 John 1:9). "O God, You know my foolishness; and my sins are not hidden from You" (Psalm 69:5). Free me from my sins, for they are a heavy burden that is "too heavy for me" (Psalm 38:4). I refuse to allow the enemy of my soul to throw guilt in my face. Your blood on the cross, Jesus, has paid the price for my sins.

In Jesus' name I pray.

Lord,
I Want to Be a
Great Parent

(Prayers from *The Power of a
Praying® Parent*)

Becoming a Praying Parent

~⁂~

Lord, may the beauty of Your Spirit be so evident in me that I will be a godly role model for my child. Teach me how to love the way You love. Give me the communication, teaching, and nurturing skills that I must have. Grow me into being the kind of parent You want me to be and teach me how to pray and truly intercede for his (her) life. I know I need You to help me. You said in Your Word, "Whatever things you ask in prayer, believing, you will receive" (Matthew 21:22). In Jesus' name I ask that You will increase my faith to believe for all the things You have put on my heart to pray for concerning my child.

In Jesus' name I pray.

Releasing My Child into God's Hands

❧

Thank You, Lord, for the precious gift of my child. Because Your Word says that every good gift comes from You, I know that You have given him (her) to me to care for and raise. Help me to do that. Show me places where I continue to hang on to him (her) and enable me to release him (her) to Your protection, guidance, and counsel. Help me not to live in fear of possible dangers, but in the joy and peace of knowing that You are in control. I'm grateful that I don't have to rely on the world's unreliable and ever-changing methods of child rearing, but that I can have clear directions from Your Word and wisdom as I pray to You for answers. I rely on You for everything, and this day I trust my child to You and release him (her) into Your hands.

In Jesus' name I pray.

Securing Protection from Harm

*L*ord, I lift (<u>name of child</u>) up to You and ask that You would put a hedge of protection around her (him). Protect her (his) spirit, body, mind, and emotions from any kind of evil or harm. I pray specifically for protection from accidents, disease, injury, or any physical, mental, or emotional abuse. Keep her (him) safe in all she (he) does and wherever she (he) goes. Protect her (him) from any hidden dangers and let no weapon formed against her (him) be able to prosper. I pray she (he) will make her (his) refuge "in the shadow of Your wings" until "these calamities have passed by" (Psalm 57:1). Hide her (him) from any kind of evil influences that would come against her (him).

In Jesus' name I pray.

Feeling Loved and Accepted

*L*ord, I pray You would help me to love my child unconditionally the way You do, and enable me to show it in a manner he (she) can perceive. Reveal to me how I can demonstrate and model Your love to him (her) so that it will be clearly understood. I pray that all my family members will love and accept him (her), and may he (she) find favor with other people as well. With each day that he (she) grows in the confidence of being loved and accepted, as he (she) comes to fully understand the depth of Your love for him (her), make him (her) a vessel through which Your love flows to others.

In Jesus' name I pray.

Establishing an Eternal Future

‿⸎⸎⸎‿

*L*ord, I bring (<u>name of child</u>) before You and ask that You would help her (him) grow into a deep understanding of who You are. Open her (his) heart and bring her (him) to a full knowledge of the truth about You. Lord, You have said in Your Word, "If you confess with your mouth the Lord Jesus and believe in your heart that God has raised Him from the dead, you will be saved" (Romans 10:9). I pray for that kind of faith for my child. May she (he) call You her (his) Savior, be filled with Your Holy Spirit, acknowledge You in every area of her (his) life, and choose always to follow You and Your ways. Help her (him) to fully believe that Jesus laid down His life for her (him) so that she (he) might have life eternally and abundantly now.

In Jesus' name I pray.

Honoring Parents and Resisting Rebellion

～～～

*L*ord, Your Word instructs, "Children, obey your parents in all things, for this is well pleasing to the Lord" (Colossians 3:20). I pray You would turn the heart of (<u>name of child</u>) toward his (her) parents and enable him (her) to honor and obey both father and mother so that his (her) life will be long and good. Turn his (her) heart toward You so that all he (she) does is pleasing in Your sight. May he (she) learn to identify and confront pride and rebellion in himself (herself) and be willing to confess and repent of it. Make him (her) uncomfortable with sin. Help him (her) to know the beauty and simplicity of walking with a sweet and humble spirit in obedience and submission to You.

In Jesus' name I pray.

Maintaining Good Family Relationships

❧

ord, I pray You would teach my child to resolve misunderstandings according to Your Word. And if any division has already begun, if any relationship is strained or severed, Lord, I pray You will drive out the wedge of division and bring healing. I pray there be no strain, breach, misunderstanding, arguing, fighting, or separating of ties. Give her (him) a heart of forgiveness and reconciliation. Your Word instructs us to "be of one mind, having compassion for one another; love as brothers, be tenderhearted, be courteous" (1 Peter 3:8). Help her (him) to live accordingly, "endeavoring to keep the unity of the Spirit in the bond of peace" (Ephesians 4:3). I pray You would instill a love and compassion in her (him) for all family members that is strong and unending, like a cord that cannot be broken.

In Jesus' name I pray.

Developing a Hunger for the Things of God

Lord, I pray for (<u>name of child</u>) to have an ever-increasing hunger for more of You. May she (he) long for Your presence—long to spend time with You in prayer, praise, and worship. Give her (him) a desire for the truth of Your Word and a love for Your laws and Your ways. Teach her (him) to live by faith and be led by the Holy Spirit, having an availability to do what You tell her (him) to do. May a deep reverence and love for You and Your ways color everything she (he) does and every choice she (he) makes. May she (he) not be wise in her (his) own eyes, but rather "fear the LORD and depart from evil" (Proverbs 3:7).

In Jesus' name I pray.

Following Truth, Rejecting Lies

⌒≈⌒

Lord, I pray You will fill (<u>name of child</u>) with Your Spirit of truth. Give her (him) a heart that loves truth and follows after it, rejecting all lies as a manifestation of the enemy. Flush out anything in her (him) that would entertain a lying spirit and cleanse her (him) from any death that has crept in as a result of lies she (he) may have spoken or thought. Help her (him) to understand that every lie gives the devil a piece of her (his) heart, and into the hole that's left comes confusion and separation from Your presence. Deliver her (him) from any lying spirit. I pray that she (he) not be blinded or deceived, but always be able to clearly understand Your truth.

In Jesus' name I pray.

Identifying God-Given Gifts and Talents

Lord, thank You for the gifts and talents You have placed in (name of child). Make them apparent to me and to her (him), and show me specifically if there is any special nurturing, training, learning experience, or opportunities I should provide for her (him). Your Word says, "Having then gifts differing according to the grace that is given to us, let us use them" (Romans 12:6). As she (he) recognizes the talents and abilities You've given her (him), I pray that no feelings of inadequacy, fear, or uncertainty will keep her (him) from using them according to Your will. May she (he) hear the call You have on her (his) life so that she (he) doesn't spend a lifetime trying to figure out what it is or miss it altogether.

In Jesus' name I pray.

Receiving a Sound Mind

*L*ord, thank You for promising us a sound mind. I lay claim to that promise for (name of child). I pray his (her) mind be clear, alert, bright, intelligent, stable, peaceful, and uncluttered. I pray there will be no confusion, no dullness, and no unbalanced, scattered, unorganized, or negative thinking. I pray that his (her) mind will not be filled with complex or confusing thoughts. Rather, give him (her) clarity of mind so that he (she) is able to think straight at all times. Give him (her) the ability to make clear decisions, to understand all he (she) needs to know, and to be able to focus on what he (she) needs to do. Where there is now any mental instability, I speak healing in Jesus' name.

In Jesus' name I pray.

Finding the Perfect Mate

*L*ord, I pray that unless Your plan is for (<u>name of child</u>) to remain single, You will send the perfect marriage partner for her (him). Send the right husband (wife) at the perfect time, and give her (him) a clear leading from You as to who it is. I pray my daughter (son) will be submissive enough to hear Your voice when it comes time to make a marriage decision, and that she (he) will make that decision based on what You are saying and not just fleshly desire. I pray she (he) will trust You with all her (his) heart and lean not on her (his) own understanding; that she (he) will acknowledge You in all her (his) ways so that You will direct her (his) path (Proverbs 3:5-6). May she (he) have one wonderful mate for life.

In Jesus' name I pray.

Seeking Wisdom and Discernment

❦

*L*ord, I pray You would give the gifts of wisdom, discernment, and revelation to (<u>name of child</u>). Help her (him) to trust You with all her (his) heart, not depending on her (his) own understanding, but acknowledging You in all her (his) ways so that she (he) may hear Your clear direction as to which path to take (Proverbs 3:5-6). Help her (him) to discern good from evil and be sensitive to the voice of the Holy Spirit saying, "This is the way, walk in it" (Isaiah 30:21). I know that much of her (his) happiness in life depends on gaining wisdom and discernment, which Your Word says brings long life, wealth, recognition, protection, enjoyment, contentment, and happiness. May all these things come to her (him) because of Your gift of wisdom.

In Jesus' name I pray.

Lord,
Show Me How to Pray
for My
Grown-Up Kids

*(Prayers from The Power of Praying®
for Your Adult Children)*

Pray That Your Adult Children Will

See God Pour Out His Spirit upon Them

~∽◦∽◦∽~

Lord, You have said that in the last days You will pour out Your Spirit upon all flesh. I cry out to You from the depths of my heart and ask that You would pour out Your Holy Spirit upon my adult children. Pour out Your Spirit upon me and my other family members as well. Pour out Your Spirit on all of my adult children's in-laws, both present and future. Pour out Your Spirit upon whatever difficult circumstances each of my adult children is facing. Be Lord over every part of their lives and every aspect of their beings. Speak to my adult children's hearts and help them to hear from You. Enable them to understand Your leading and direction for their lives.

In Jesus' name I pray.

Pray That Your Adult Children Will

Develop a Heart for God, His Word, and His Ways

꧁~꧂

Lord, I pray (<u>name of adult child</u>) will love Your Word and will feed her (his) soul with it every day. Speak to her (his) heart and breathe life into every word so that it comes alive to her (him). Teach her (him) Your ways and Your laws and enable her (him) to do the right thing. I pray a silencing of the enemy's voice so that she (he) will hear the Holy Spirit speaking to her (his) heart. You have said in Your Word that when someone turns his ear away from hearing the law, even his prayer is an abomination (Proverbs 28:9). I pray that she (he) will never turn a deaf ear to Your laws.

In Jesus' name I pray.

Pray That Your Adult Children Will

Grow in Wisdom, Discernment, and Revelation

❧

ord, I pray (<u>name of adult child</u>) will have wisdom that comes through Your Holy Spirit (1 Corinthians 12:8). Help him (her) to be strong, refusing to fall into the ways of the foolish. Help him (her) to have the wisdom to never blaspheme Your name. Bring strong conviction into his (her) heart whenever he (she) is tempted. Instead, I pray he (she) will "let the high praises of God" be in his (her) mouth and "a two-edged sword" in his (her) hand (Psalm 149:6). Give him (her) wisdom that guides him (her) away from danger and protects him (her) from evil. Give him (her) a deep sense of the truth, and the ability to take information and make accurate judgments about it.

In Jesus' name I pray.

Pray That Your Adult Children Will

Understand God's Purpose for Their Lives

❧❦❧

Lord, I pray for (<u>name of adult child</u>) to have a sense of purpose for his (her) life and the ability to understand that purpose with clarity. Give him (her) the Spirit of wisdom and revelation so that the eyes of his (her) understanding will be enlightened. Help him (her) to know what is the hope of Your calling and what is the exceeding greatness of Your power on his (her) behalf (Ephesians 1:17-19). I pray Your plans to fulfill the destiny and purpose You have for him (her) will succeed, and not the plans of the enemy. Enable him (her) to separate himself (herself) from all the distractions of this world and turn to You in order to hear Your voice.

In Jesus' name I pray.

Pray That Your Adult Children Will

Work Successfully and Have Financial Stability

⟨⟨⟨∼∙∽⟩⟩⟩

*L*ord, I pray Your blessings upon (<u>name of adult child</u>). Bless the work of her (his) hands in every way. Give her (him) a strong sense of purpose so that she (he) is led to the right occupation and is always in the job or position that is Your will for her (his) life. Speak to her (him) about what she (he) was created to do, so that she (he) never wanders from job to job without a purpose. Help her (him) find great purpose in every job she (he) does. Pour out Your Holy Spirit upon her (him) and help her (him) to be "not lagging in diligence, fervent in spirit, serving the Lord" (Romans 12:11).

In Jesus' name I pray.

Pray That Your Adult Children Will

Resist Evil Influences and Destructive Behavior

~~~

*L*ord, I pray You will give (<u>name of adult child</u>) the discernment she (he) needs to understand the clear choice between good and evil, and right and wrong, between what is life giving and life destroying, and between a path into a secure and good future and a dead-end street. I pray that she (he) will not allow the world to shape her (him), but instead she (he) would be shaped by You. I know that the influence of the enemy can come in so subtly as to be nearly unobserved until it's too late. But I pray that with Holy Spirit–given wisdom and discernment she (he) can be prepared for the enemy and anticipate his plans.

In Jesus' name I pray.

Pray That Your Adult Children Will

Avoid All Sexual Pollution and Temptation

~~~~~~~

*L*ord, help my adult child to flee sexual pollution—to turn away from it, not look at it, and not be drawn into it. Give him (her) the conviction to change the channel; shut down the website; throw out the magazine, DVD, or CD; or walk out of the theater (Proverbs 27:12). Give him (her) understanding that any deviation from the path You have for him (her)—even if it is only occurring in the mind—will be a trap to fall into and a snare for his (her) soul. Enable him (her) to stand on the solid ground of purity in Your sight. Help him (her) to hide Your Word in his (her) heart so that he (she) will not sin against You (Psalm 119:9-11).

In Jesus' name I pray.

Pray That Your Adult Children Will

Experience God's Healing

~~~

*L*ord, I pray (<u>name of adult child</u>) will learn to pray in power for her (his) own healing. Raise up in her (him) great faith in the name of Jesus. Give her (him) the understanding to claim the healing that was achieved at the cross. Any place in her (his) body where there is sickness, disease, infirmity, or injury, I pray You would touch her (him) and bring complete healing. Help her (him) to not give up praying until she (he) sees the total healing You have for her (him). Whether her (his) healing is instantaneous or it manifests in a gradual recuperation, I thank You in advance for the miracle of healing You will do in her (him) body.

In Jesus' name I pray.

Pray That Your Adult Children Will

Experience Good Health

*L*ord, I pray (<u>name of adult child</u>) will enjoy good health and a long life. Give her (him) the wisdom and knowledge necessary to recognize that her (his) body is the temple of Your Holy Spirit and that it should be cared for and nurtured and not disregarded or mistreated. Help her (him) to value good health as a gift from You to be protected and not squandered on foolish or careless living or taken for granted. Teach her (him) how to make wise choices and to reject anything that undermines good health. Reveal any truth that needs to be seen, and give her (him) understanding. Teach her (him) to be disciplined in the way of eating, exercising, and getting proper rest.

In Jesus' name I pray.

Pray That Your Adult Children Will

Enjoy a Successful Marriage and Raise Godly Children

❧

Lord, I pray for (name of adult child) and ask that You would give him (her) the perfect wife (husband). Bring a godly believing woman (man) into his (her) life, who will be with him (her) for the rest of their lives in a fulfilling and happy marriage. I pray that she (he) will have purity of heart, plus a nature and character that is gracious, kind, giving, and loving. I pray that they will always be attracted to one another in a way that is lasting. I pray above all that they will have great and lasting love for one another. Dwell in their marriage, Lord, and make it what You want it to be.

In Jesus' name I pray.

Pray That Your Adult Children Will
Maintain Strong and Fulfilling Relationships

~~⊱•⊰~~

Lord, I pray (<u>name of adult child</u>) will have friends who tell her (him) the truth in love (Proverbs 27:6). I pray for friends who are wise (Proverbs 13:20) and will always be a strong support for her (him) (Ecclesiastes 4:9-10). I pray that each relationship in her (his) life will be glorifying to You. I pray also for good relationships with parents, siblings, and other family members. Bless these relationships with deep love, great compassion, mutual understanding, and good communication. Where there are breaches or rough spots in any one of those relationships, I pray You would bring peace, healing, and reconciliation. I pray that the enemy will not be able to break apart any relationships or friendships.

In Jesus' name I pray.

Pray That Your Adult Children Will

Be Protected and Survive Tough Times

_{~⚬⚯⚬~}

Lord, I pray You would surround my adult children with Your angels to keep watch over them so that they will not stumble (Psalm 91:12). Help them to hear Your voice leading them, and teach them to obey You so that they will always be in Your will and at the right place at the right time. I pray that "the fear of the LORD" will be for them a "fountain of life" that will serve to turn them "away from the snares of death" (Proverbs 14:27). I pray You will keep Your eyes on them and that they will not take their eyes off of You. Help them to learn to dwell in Your shadow where they are protected (Psalm 91:1).

In Jesus' name I pray.

Recognize Their Need for God

Lord, I pray for (name of adult child) that You would help her (him) recognize her (his) need for You. Help her (him) to understand that You know her (his) needs even better than she (he) does (Luke 12:29-30). Teach her (him) to seek You as her (his) hiding place and hope (Psalm 119:114). Strengthen her (him) to choose to keep Your commandments and "depart" from those who would lead her (him) away from You (Psalm 119:115). I pray You would teach her (him) Your ways—"as Your custom is toward those who love Your name" (Psalm 119:124,132). Help me to live Your way and to model clearly what utter dependence on You looks like, so she (he) will be inspired to walk in that same way (1 John 5:2).

In Jesus' name I pray.

Pray That Your Adult Children Will

Walk into the Future God Has for Them

❦

Lord, I pray for (<u>name of adult child</u>) to have a future that is good, long, prosperous, and secure because it is in Your hands. Thank You that Your thoughts toward him (her) are thoughts of peace and to give him (her) a future and a hope (Jeremiah 29:11). Turn his (her) heart toward You so that he (she) always has Your will and Your ways in mind. Keep him (her) from wasting time on a pathway that You will not bless. Help him (her) to run the race in the right way, so that he (she) will finish strong and receive the prize You have for him (her) (1 Corinthians 9:24). I pray that nothing will ever separate him (her) from You (Romans 8:38-39).

In Jesus' name I pray.

Lord,
Thank You for the Presence of Your Spirit in My Life

(Prayers from *Lead Me, Holy Spirit*)

Led to Receive the Relationship with God You Have Always Needed

Lord, help me to know You more. Enable me to fully understand my relationship with You through Jesus, Your Son. Help me, Jesus, to comprehend all You accomplished for me on the cross. Thank You for Your suffering and death, which have saved me from the consequences of my own wrong thoughts and actions. I am eternally grateful that after You were crucified, You rose from the dead to prove that You are who You say You are and that Your words and promises are without fail. I declare that You are Lord over every aspect of my life. Thank You for forgiving me of all my sins, giving me a new beginning and the promise of eternity with You.

In Jesus' name I pray.

Led to Receive the Freedom and Wholeness God Has for You

Lord, help me to receive the wholeness You have for me. Free me from everything that keeps me from becoming all You created me to be. Thank You, Holy Spirit, that I can find liberty in Your presence (2 Corinthians 3:17). Liberate me from anything in me or around me that is not Your will for my life. Set me free from every evil work. Quiet my mind, cleanse my heart, heal every negative emotion, and set me free from anything that is not of You. Thank You that You will continue to deliver me until I am completely whole. Enable me to stand strong against ever falling back into any kind of bondage or error again.

In Jesus' name I pray.

Led to Receive the Inheritance Laid Up for You as God's Child

⚜

Lord, thank You that You are my heavenly Father and You have made me to be Your child (1 John 3:1). I am grateful for the inheritance You have given me and that You have made me to be a joint heir with Christ. Help me to understand all that this means and how I am to possess what You have for my life. Holy Spirit, I come before You and ask You to speak to my heart about whatever I need to know. Show me what You want me to see. Enable me to follow Your leading as I move into this holy inheritance and open up to everything You have provided for my life.

In Jesus' name I pray.

Led to Be Filled with His Wisdom and Revelation

❦

Lord, I thank You for Your Holy Spirit of wisdom and revelation living in me. Thank You that Your wisdom gives me common sense and the ability to make wise decisions and choices. I pray for wisdom in all things. Thank You that You give wisdom to those who ask You for it (James 1:5). Help me to always seek Your wisdom and not the wisdom of the world and to clearly know the difference. I pray that I will have the wisdom I need in order to stay safe and free from the "way of evil" (Proverbs 2:10-12). Reveal to me all the things I must understand. Give me the revelation I need when I need it.

In Jesus' name I pray.

Led to Be Filled with His Love and Hope

〜⌘〜

*L*ord, I thank You for Your Spirit of love dwelling in my heart so that I am ever filled with hope. Help me to comprehend the width, length, depth, and height of Your love (Ephesians 3:18). Enable me to continuously receive the love of Christ which passes all understanding so that I may be filled with all the fullness of God (Ephesians 3:19). Teach me to love others the way You do. I know that though I speak like an angel, but I don't have love, I'm just making noise; and if I have the faith to move a mountain, but I don't have love, "I am nothing" (1 Corinthians 13:1-2). Spirit of love and hope, flow powerfully through me at all times.

In Jesus' name I pray.

Led to Hear God's Word in Your Mind

Lord, I ask that Your Holy Spirit, who inspired the writing of the Scriptures, will bring Your Word alive in my heart every time I read or hear it. Help me to retain it. Prepare me with Your Word so that I am complete and thoroughly equipped for everything You have for me to do. Make Your Word become part of the fabric of my being. Weave it into my soul so that it forms who I am. Help me to hear Your voice speaking to me every time I read it. Don't let me neglect Your law and cause my prayers to become an abomination to You (Proverbs 28:9). I want to live in the peace You have for those who love Your ways (Psalm 119:165).

In Jesus' name I pray.

Led to Hear God's Voice Speaking to Your Heart

~~~

*L*ord, help me to hear Your voice speaking to me when I read Your Word so that I can recognize Your voice speaking to my heart at other times as well. I know You care about the details of my life, so I ask You to help me understand when You are giving me specific directions. Keep me from moving on something before I know what You are leading me to do. If there are words You want me to speak to another person, give me the "tongue of the learned" so that I will "know how to speak a word in season to him who is weary" (Isaiah 50:4). Teach me to hear Your voice and follow Your leading in my life.

In Jesus' name I pray.

Led to Worship with Your Whole Heart

❧

*L*ord, I don't want to be a weak, ineffective, or halfhearted worshipper of You. You are everything to me. I don't want to be like the people in Your Word who had it all—Your presence and Your Holy Spirit with them—and they lost it because their hearts were far from You. Teach me to worship You with my whole heart—with everything that is in me. "My soul follows close behind You" (Psalm 63:8). I don't want my worship to ever reflect anything but total reverence for You. Forgive me for any time I have not given You all the worship You deserve. Help me to make worship of You the first place I run to when I have concerns.

In Jesus' name I pray.

Led to Be Separate from the World

❧

Lord, help me to be separate from the world and yet still be in it in an effective way to do Your will. Show me how to live in this world and be Your light extended without being drawn into and influenced by all that is dark and dangerous to my life. Strengthen me to reject all peer pressure to be anything other than who You made me to be. Show me where I have given in to certain practices in the culture that are not pleasing to You. Help me to shut off or shut down anything that is polluting my mind. Open my eyes to things I have become accustomed to that I should not have.

In Jesus' name I pray.

Led to See Purpose in Your Reason for Getting Up Every Day

Lord, help me to be filled with a sense of Your love, joy, peace, and purpose every morning when I get up. Enable me to know with all certainty that You are with me and I am not alone. Strengthen my faith to understand without doubt that You, Holy Spirit, will guide me every step of my way. Help me to see Your purpose for my life so that I will stay on the right path. Where my vision for Your purpose in my life has become blurred, give me clarity. My soul waits on You, Lord, more than those who watch for the morning (Psalm 130:5-6). Thank You, Lord, that You "will perfect that which concerns me" (Psalm 138:8).

In Jesus' name I pray.

Led to See Purpose in the Gifts God Has Put in You

Lord, I pray You would reveal to me the gifts and talents You have put in me. Enable me to understand their value to You. Where the gifts I want don't line up with the gifts I have, help me to submit those desires to You and allow You to be in control. Develop the gifts You have put in me so that they become useful for Your kingdom. Teach me to move in excellence with them, always knowing that I have not perfected them, but it is You who have done it. I pray that any insecurity in me—which I know is actually a lack of faith in Your ability to guide and sustain me—will not rule over my using the gifts You have placed in me.

In Jesus' name I pray.

Led to Pray for as Long as It Takes

*L*ord, I pray You will help me to not give up praying when I don't see answers to my prayers right away or because my prayers are not answered exactly the way I prayed them. Regarding the things that are most pressing on my heart, enable me to pray for as long as it takes. Help me to not grow weary in doing good, for I know that "in due season we shall reap if we do not lose heart" (Galatians 6:9). Thank You that You always hear and always answer—in Your way and Your time. I have set You always before me, Lord, and because You are with me, I shall not give up (Psalm 16:8).

In Jesus' name I pray.

Led to Follow God to the Right Place at the Right Time

Lead me, Holy Spirit, into everything You have for me today. Guide me to the place I should be. Help me to not resist Your direction or, worse yet, to miss hearing You entirely. When there are times that it is hard to determine what the right thing is, reveal it to me by Your Spirit. Help me to do what is good in Your sight, Lord, so that it may be well with me, and that I can go in and possess all that You have for me (Deuteronomy 6:18). I want to always be in the right place at the right time, and I know that is not possible unless I follow the leading of Your Spirit and I wait for Your direction.

In Jesus' name I pray.

Led to Lead Others to Find Hope in the Lord

✦

Lord, help me to communicate the hope I have in You to others who need to hear about it. Teach me to sense when someone is discouraged and hopeless. Enable me to "always be ready to give a defense to everyone who asks" me about my reason for the hope within me (1 Peter 3:15). Enable me to lead others to see the hope they have in You, as well. I know Your eye is on those who fear You and who put their hope in You and Your mercy (Psalm 33:18). I commit to You as a laborer in Your field and say, "I will hope continually, and will praise You yet more and more" (Psalm 71:14).

In Jesus' name I pray.

Lord,
I Want to Reflect Your Heart

(Prayers from *The Power of a*
Praying® *Woman*)

Lord, Draw Me into a Closer Walk with You

❧

Lord, I draw close to You today, grateful that You will draw close to me as You have promised in Your Word (James 4:8). I long to dwell in Your presence, and I want to know You in every way You can be known. Teach me what I need to learn in order to know You better. I don't want to be a person who is "always learning and never able to come to the knowledge of the truth" (2 Timothy 3:7). I want to know the truth about who You are because I know that You are near to all who call upon You in truth (Psalm 145:18). Draw me close as I draw near to you, so that I may dwell in Your presence like never before.

In Jesus' name I pray.

Lord, Cleanse Me and Make My Heart Right Before You

Lord, I come humbly before You and ask You to cleanse my heart and renew a right spirit within me. Forgive me for thoughts I have had, words I have spoken, and things that I have done that are not glorifying to You or are in direct contradiction to Your commands. Specifically, I confess to You (<u>name any thoughts, words, or actions that you know are not pleasing to God</u>). I confess it as sin and I repent of it. I choose to walk away from this pattern of thought or action and live Your way. I know that You are "gracious and merciful, slow to anger and of great kindness" (Joel 2:13). Forgive me for ever taking that for granted.

In Jesus' name I pray.

Lord, Help Me to Be a Forgiving Person

Lord, help me to be a forgiving person. Show me where I am not. If I have any anger, bitterness, resentment, or unforgiveness that I am not recognizing, reveal it to me and I will confess it to You as sin. Specifically, I ask You to help me fully forgive (<u>name anyone you feel you need to forgive</u>). Make me to understand the depth of Your forgiveness toward me so that I won't hold back forgiveness from others. I realize that my forgiving someone doesn't make them right; it makes me free. I also realize that You are the only one who knows the whole story, and You will see justice done.

In Jesus' name I pray.

Lord, Strengthen Me to Stand Against the Enemy

❧

Lord, I thank You for suffering and dying on the cross for me and for rising again to defeat death and hell. My enemy is defeated because of what You have done. Thank You that You have given me all authority over him (Luke 10:19). Show me when I am not recognizing the encroachment of the enemy in my life. Teach me to use that authority You have given me to see him defeated in every area. Help me to fast and pray regularly in order to break any stronghold the enemy is trying to erect in my life. By the power of Your Holy Spirit I can successfully resist the devil and he must flee from me (James 4:7).

In Jesus' name I pray.

Lord, Show Me How to Take Control of My Mind

❦

*L*ord, I don't ever want to walk according to my own thinking (Isaiah 65:2). I want to bring every thought captive and control my mind. Your Word is "a discerner of the thoughts and intents of the heart" (Hebrews 4:12). As I read Your Word, may it reveal any wrong thinking in me. May Your Word be so etched in my mind that I will be able to identify a lie of the enemy the minute I hear it. Spirit of truth, keep me undeceived. I know You have given me authority "over all the power of the enemy" (Luke 10:19), and so I command the enemy to get away from my mind. I refuse to listen to lies.

In Jesus' name I pray.

Lord, Take Me Deeper in Your Word

Lord, "Your Word is a lamp to my feet and a light to my path" (Psalm 119:105). Enable me to truly comprehend its deepest meaning. Give me greater understanding than I have ever had before, and reveal to me the hidden treasures buried there. I pray that I will have a heart that is teachable and open to what You want me to know. Change me as I read it. Help me to be diligent to put Your Word inside my soul faithfully every day. Show me where I'm wasting time that could be better spent reading Your Word. Give me the ability to memorize it. Etch it in my mind and heart so that it becomes a part of me.

In Jesus' name I pray.

Lord, Instruct Me as I Put My Life in Right Order

Lord, I pray You would help me set my life in right order. I want to always put You first above all else in my life. Teach me how to love You with all my heart, mind, and soul. Show me when I am not doing that. Show me if I have lifted up my soul to an idol. My desire is to serve You and only You. Please help me to live accordingly. Give me a submissive heart. Help me to always submit to the governing authorities and the correct people in my family, work, and church. Show me who the proper spiritual authorities are to be in my life. Plant me in the church You want me to be in.

In Jesus' name I pray.

Lord, Plant Me So I Will Bear the Fruit of Your Spirit

❧

Lord, I pray You would plant the fruit of Your Spirit in me and cause it to flourish. Help me to abide in You, Jesus, so that I will bear fruit in my life. Holy Spirit, fill me afresh with Your love today so that it will flow out of me and into the lives of others. You said in Your Word to "let the peace of Christ rule in your hearts" (Colossians 3:15). I pray that Your peace would rule my heart and mind to such a degree that people would sense it when they are around me. Help me to "pursue the things which make for peace and the things by which one may edify another" (Romans 14:19).

In Jesus' name I pray.

Lord, Move Me into the Purpose for Which I Was Created

❧

*L*ord, I know Your plan for me existed before I knew You, and You will bring it to pass. Help me to "walk worthy of the calling with which [I was] called" (Ephesians 4:1). I know there is an appointed plan for me, and I have a destiny that will now be fulfilled. Help me to live my life with a sense of purpose and understanding of the calling You have given me. Take away any discouragement I may feel and replace it with joyful anticipation of what You are going to do through me. Use me as Your instrument to make a positive difference in the lives of those whom You put in my path.

In Jesus' name I pray.

Lord, Guide Me in All My Relationships

Lord, I lift up every one of my relationships to You and ask You to bless them. I ask that Your peace would reign in them and that each one would be glorifying to You. Help me to choose my friends wisely so I won't be led astray. Give me discernment and strength to separate myself from anyone who is not a good influence. I release all my relationships to You and pray Your will be done in each one of them. I especially pray for my relationship with each of my family members. I pray You would bring healing, reconciliation, and restoration where it is needed. Bless these relationships and make them strong.

In Jesus' name I pray.

Lord, Set Me Free from Negative Emotions

Lord, help me to live in Your joy and peace. Give me strength and understanding to resist anxiety, anger, envy, depression, bitterness, hopelessness, loneliness, fear, and guilt. Rescue me when "my spirit is overwhelmed within me; my heart within me is distressed" (Psalm 143:4). I refuse to let my life be brought down by negative emotions such as these. When I am tempted to give in to them, show me Your truth. You have said in Your Word that by our patience we can possess our souls (Luke 21:19). Give me patience so I can do that. Help me to keep my "heart with all diligence," for I know that "out of it spring the issues of life" (Proverbs 4:23).

In Jesus' name I pray.

Lord, Lift Me out of My Past

❧

*L*ord, I pray You would set me free from my past. Wherever I have made the past my home, I pray You would deliver me, heal me, and redeem me from it. Help me to let go of anything I have held onto of my past that has kept me from moving into all You have for me. Enable me to put off all former ways of thinking and feeling and remembering (Ephesians 4:22-24). Give me the mind of Christ so I will be able to understand when I am being controlled by memories of past events. I release my past to You and everyone associated with it so You can restore what has been lost.

In Jesus' name I pray.

Lord, Lead Me into the Future You Have for Me

⸺❧⸺

Lord, I put my future in Your hands and ask that You would give me total peace about it. I want to be in the center of Your plans for my life, knowing You have given me everything I need for what is ahead. I pray You would give me strength to endure without giving up. You have said that "he who endures to the end will be saved" (Matthew 10:22). Help me to run the race in a way that I shall finish strong and receive the prize You have for me (1 Corinthians 9:24). Help me to be always watchful in my prayers, because I don't know when the end of my life will be (1 Peter 4:7).

In Jesus' name I pray.

Lord,
Help Me Love You and Others in a Way That Pleases You

(Prayers from *Choose Love*)

See Yourself the Way God Sees You

*L*ord, help me to see myself the way You see me. Thank You that You see me through Your eyes of love and all You created me to be. Enable me to open up my heart to receive Your love. Although it's hard to comprehend a love so great, and I don't feel worthy of it, I don't want to shut myself off from the power of Your amazing love working in my heart. Give me eyes to see how You reveal Your love for me by keeping me from things that are not Your greatest good for my life. I know that everything You want to do in my life cannot be accomplished without Your love flowing in me.

In Jesus' name I pray.

Understand Who God Really Is

ord, I long to know You better. Teach me all about You. I know I cannot begin to comprehend Your greatness without Your opening my eyes, enlarging my heart and mind, and giving me revelation. "O LORD my God, You are very great: You are clothed with honor and majesty, who cover Yourself with light as with a garment, who stretch out the heavens like a curtain" (Psalm 104:1-2). Help me to understand all that You are so that I can grow ever deeper in my walk with You. You are the all-knowing Creator of all things, and You can transform anyone with Your love if they will receive it. I open my heart fully to You and ask You to transform me.

In Jesus' name I pray.

Receive All God Has for You

Lord, I realize I can never receive all You have for me until I understand everything You did for me. Thank You that You, "the ruler over the kings of the earth," loved me enough to wash me clean of all my sins by Your own blood (Revelation 1:5). Thank You that You are the living Word. You are my Savior. You have set me free from the consequences of my own sins, errors, mistakes, and ignorance. And You have made me to be a beloved child of God. Thank You that receiving Your love for me has caused my life to finally make sense. Thank You that in You I find everything I need for life (1 Corinthians 8:6).

In Jesus' name I pray.

Read God's Love Letter to You

*L*ord, thank You for Your Word. I know it's Your love letter to me because every time I read or speak it, I experience Your presence and love in a deeper way. It feeds my soul and makes my life rich. Help me to understand it better every day. "Open my eyes, that I may see wondrous things from Your law" (Psalm 119:18). Help me to know You in greater depth through it. Thank You that Your Word gives me truth and guidance for my life. Help me to always keep Your Word in my heart and not forget it. Make the Scriptures come alive to me every time I read them. Keep them alive in me at all times.

In Jesus' name I pray.

Accept God's Grace and Mercy

*L*ord, thank You for Your grace and mercy, which I know are never-ending signs of Your unfailing love for me. They are gifts beyond comprehension. For it is You who redeems my life from destruction and crowns me "with loving kindness and tender mercies" (Psalm 103:4). Thank You that You care about the things I care about. Thank You that You "will perfect that which concerns me; Your mercy, O LORD, endures forever" (Psalm 138:8). That means I can always depend on it. Thank You that because I have received Jesus I have been forgiven, but You have promised to forgive even the sins I commit in the future when I come to You with a repentant heart and confess them.

In Jesus' name I pray.

Recognize the Ways God Loves You

*L*ord, thank You for all of the ways You love me. I recognize them more and more. I am so grateful that nothing will separate me from Your love. Thank You that Your Word promises to those in need that "in the days of famine" we will "be satisfied" (Psalm 37:19). I don't have to fear not having enough, and I can trust that because You are my Lord, I will not want for anything (Psalm 23:1). Thank You that You have a place of rest for me where there is fruitful abundance (Psalm 23:2). Thank You that You will not withhold any good thing from those who live Your way (Psalm 84:11).

In Jesus' name I pray.

Know What God's Love Will Do in Your Life

*L*ord, I am amazed at what You can and will do in me because You love me. Help me to understand the expanse of Your reach into my life. Enable me to remember this when I am in the middle of a storm and need You to bring calm (Psalm 107:28-29). Thank You that You can turn a wilderness into a pool of refreshing water (Psalm 107:35). Thank You that You always see me and know where I am. I am grateful that because I have invited You to be Lord over my life, Your hand is always upon me and will guide me where I need to go. Thank You that because I am with You, You are always with me.

In Jesus' name I pray.

Love Who He Is Wholeheartedly

~~~

*L*ord, I love who You are and all You have done for me. I love all Your promises to me and everything You have planned for my future. Reveal to me any place in my life where I am not depending on You as I should. I am eternally grateful to be an heir of Your kingdom that You have given to those who love You (James 2:5). But even more than all of that, I simply want to love You with all my heart, soul, mind, and strength just as You desire (Mark 12:30). Help me to love You with my entire being, without compromise. Teach me how to accomplish that in every way that is pleasing to You.

In Jesus' name I pray.

Lean on His Wisdom Enthusiastically

*L*ord, I love that Your wisdom is eternal, true, and always perfect. Help me to seek out and depend on Your wisdom every day and not the wisdom of the world. I reverence You and thank You that Your wisdom in me begins there. Thank You that Your law is in my heart and will keep me from slipping. I seek Your wisdom for every day and every decision. Holy Spirit of wisdom, fill me afresh with Your wisdom so that I can always hear Your wise counsel spoken to my heart. I depend on Your counsel for all things. Teach me to value that all my days on earth so I may gain a heart of wisdom (Psalm 90:12).

In Jesus' name I pray.

Is Consistently Loving Others Really Possible?

⟨❧⟩

Lord, I know that without You I don't have it in me to love others the way You want me to. It's only because of Your healing and restoring love guiding me by the power of Your Spirit that I have the capacity and the strength to show love in a life-changing way. I pray You would pour Your love into my heart and give me the ability to love people the way You do. Enable me to always show love in a manner that's pleasing to You. I know that my love for others can reveal Your perfect love within me. Help me to always be available to Your enabling me to do exactly that.

In Jesus' name I pray.

Isn't It Selfish to Learn to Love Myself?

ord, thank You that You love me and that You made me for Your purposes. Help me to appreciate all You have put in me. Enable me to recognize the gifts You have given me to be used for Your glory. Teach me to see the good in me that I'm not seeing and help me to reject any self-criticism I focus on. Teach me to love You more and love myself better so I can express love to others with greater clarity. Help me to seek wisdom that comes only from You because I care enough about myself to become all You made me to be. Help me to understand how much You love me and what You see in me.

In Jesus' name I pray.

How Can I Show Love in Every Situation?

*L*ord, I pursue love just as I pursue You, because You are love and Your love never fails. Fill my heart so full of Your love that it overflows to others. Enable me to show Your love in every situation. I depend on You for guidance with that. Lead me by Your Holy Spirit to make decisions regarding what is always pleasing to You. I don't want to interfere with what You are doing in another's life. I don't want to move in the flesh, but instead be led by Your Spirit in all I do and say. Help me to seek Your will in every situation and with each person, and not assume I know what to do in every case.

In Jesus' name I pray.